PRAISE FOR *SEVERAL DE*

'[I]ntellectual force and ambition, language always taut and lively and fun for the reader. Nightmare whispers, musical echoes, emotional truths, collide; the poems have each their own stance, and the book opens on an ocean of voices.'

— Eiléan Ní Chuilleanáin

'Never was so much meaning packed into small verses; pour the oils of reading on almost anything in this collection and whole worlds mushroom. It is annoyingly impressive and, I must say, I hate this young fellow whatever club he's playing at tonight. [...] *Several Deer* is such a mixture of irony and malaprop, of MacNeice splendour and Audenesque knowingness, that it will annoy as many readers as it thrills. But I'm in Crothers' fan club, I have to say, and I would never want to refute a poet like this, a poet of the new post-Troubles era, who, unmistakably assembled on Ulster soil, has been given a metallic spray-job in some garage near the English fens.'

— Thomas McCarthy, *Trumpet*

'This is poetry at its most playful, sonorous and broad but also technical and intricately textured. It is poetry that compels itself forward with a terrific energy born out of appearing as though it might at any moment fall flat on its face.'

— Nathan Ellis, *The London Magazine*

'Adam Crothers' *Several Deer* is that rare thing, a genuinely enjoyable poetry collection. It is also, in places, very funny. [...] Sources as disparate as The Sensations and Robert Herrick get mashed together into goofball sonnets and villanelles. And yet for all its wit and brio, there is great seriousness to his work. Crothers is a worthy addition to yet another *nouvelle vague* of brilliant young poets from Northern Ireland.'

— Conor O'Callaghan

THE CULTURE OF MY STUFF

ADAM CROTHERS

CARCANET

First published in Great Britain in 2020 by
Carcanet
Alliance House, 30 Cross Street
Manchester M2 7AQ
www.carcanet.co.uk

A CIP catalogue record for this book is
available from the British Library.
ISBN 978 1 78410 951 6

Book design by Andrew Latimer
Printed in Great Britain by SRP Ltd, Exeter, Devon

The publisher acknowledges financial
assistance from Arts Council England.

Contents

III   FUTURES

For Rosalind

I
CULTURE

EASTER WINGS

Lord, this wasn't meant to be. I think you should see
the other guy. He keeps the beat and larks harmoniously.

I didn't plummet, plagued, from your sub-par rosy ring.
All it was for me was a gradual process of razoring

off the frills I unrequired. Another decade
and I'll be okay with being nothing: all boxes unticked

on the census, the grant proposal, the dating app.
My stance is clear of adored. My mind's the gap.

My thighs are limited. The two sets of footprints are from when
I carried you and somebody came over to ask what was going on.

I left you on the beach, an ickle squiggle. Don't you look fancy.
It wouldn't be fair. Comfort's best served cold; hence I

became most unthin, unthinkably. This wasn't ordained
to be taken orally or at face value. But there, I've done it. &?

DAMAE PLURES

Even as the roebuck and the hart is eaten, so thou shalt eat them:
the unclean and the clean shall eat of them alike.
DEUTERONOMY 12:22

I   MUNTJAC

Scoop of green scrap in the streetlamp's wee-streak
splash zone. Small and mossy doggish flatline.
Crucifixion-scenic, an asterisk
of limb; a footered reference. That lane's

for bike folk, who yelp *What the actual*
at the death cycle. I damn their buck eyes
and go home where the values are tactile.
Home, where the books require many boxes.

I cut off my face, which really spites it.
I hole up in the culture of my stuff
while 'muntjac' autocorrects to 'account'.

It is, I suppose, settled. The night's stick
snaps beneath a beautiful frigid hoof.
Faith, frighted, yields what little ground was gained.

II   CERNUNNOS

Congratulations on the roadkill verse
and all, my boy; pray, where's my boy's award?
The boy is away with the various
vocabularies of being away.

Vocabularies of an absent god.
The raising of two sons and the rain on
the side door you would take now if you could.
A loss, a lock; it's good to torc. Ring, ring.

Oh loose the lough upon the leafy sub-
urb: Tayto salad days' slaw of despond
washed as from a petroglyph mould-peppered,

in nomine patris who'd better save
his handsome worries for the older son,
the one who always was so good with words.

Swamp, drain! Guts, churn. Brag, vain tongue, in twelve-tone
waltz time. Gimp-maimed, yet you bring 'leven un-
even walls down. Scrimp, saved. Gods earn big when
ten men delve. Nine faultlines crimp lands that aren't

rich; wind lessens, grieving. Eight tonnes scrimshaw,
good for bricks: van burns, unhelped. Darn. What's done?
Scrimshave. Cut cornflakes. Whet them on seven
whetstones. Six brave guests can raze what thumbs deem

safe. Doughnuts, five; shrimp plate; catch four brides, faint-
ing. Intestinal tide, wimps. Dave, get Schoen-
berg's enema; Niamh, find salts: I'm glimpse-lamed,

guys. Check bravado: none. Define 'cult': mine.
Stamp page. Gate, barred. Three. Then open valve. Two.
Scald. One at which point the doe's voice decays.

IV   ACTAEON

Another's musk's the best thing about it,
the ghost-sack you scrub, and yet you ablute
with most rabid foam. Soap-bubble-beaded,
the lace of hair that isn't yours seems wrought

that one might leash the dogs of war and walk
them, gentrified, about your piecemeal mound,
your stack of merchandise and swag. Your wig
is unprofound: tip not that hat, straw man.

Tip otherwise, and render void your till.
Inscribe upon its vaults EMPTIED DAILY.
Id est, love more. The polling stats suggest

'forgiveness' sounds divine. Though I've heard tell
you rest less when you've let somebody lie,
and then you set the hounds upon yourself.

V   VAMPIRE

Impaled received invoices on one prong,
outgoing t'other, it takes your luggage,
overbites the straps; rank nature, pulling,
stakes on its minted breath, it stinks of cash,

the servile fawn that drags your bags through grooves,
through deep dull platitudes. It looks like death
has no dominion: check out the rough
beat clocking the hallway, pulsing with math.

You wake at midnight, probably, your jeans
on and your heart skinned. A convoy of trucks,
or zones of snowless dirt: black box, black box,

little black box. Dang swell to imagine
removing staples from redacted docs
a labour suited to the cervid's tusks.

VI   BAMBI

for Kesha Rose Sebert

The Silence of Hearts and the Noise of Clubs,
the Void of Diamonds and the Blank of Spades
are spiked on briars by which your head is cupped.
Of steel and tinsel are the antlers made.

You can't see the cards, yet guess who you are.
Some say different. You butt in the rut
the brink's wall and do all in your power
to have a twig give up a flower. Right?

Right. There blossoms but a recoil, a rep-
ort: *the meadow is burning and what to*
do the meadow is burning so much for

you... Run along, Eirene. How'd you sleep
last night? You charge again. And there's glitter
on the floor, and there's glitter on the floor.

Thought you were done. Thought the Cailleach Bhéara'd
plant grand snowcaps in the gap between us.
So much depends upon her wheelbarrow
that by my troth I cannot even. As

if I would, could I. Person/not-person
strobes distantly, gloves out to catch release.
Gloves rammed at their wrists through a skull. Reson-
ant in valleys, what hurt herds heard. Aural's

the tricksiest: your lobe-splitting whisper...
Have, please, what you need of me. Take a knee.
Heed no grave shadow of an appetite

that walks those hypothetical hills. For
we're sorry-sated, well read, fallow. Now,
having been so rudely interrupted.

ORDERING A MUDSLIDE

Be not afraid. Or do be, do. The rallying cry is your call,
perhaps your last. Poised at the bar, a variety of wall,

little I spies mud sliding out of the shaker, the cold war drum
where the Irish cream their clean green jeans as in a dream,

a dream of Mexico and Russia in mixed moods double-teaming
an already-melting lack of meaning. An iceberg, besotted, scheming

to be sated, shapeless. I was kind of thinking
maybe it could rape less. Celebratory drink-clinking

has wounded the side of the glass that is my saviour. It's blasphemy,
but the cloaca of the aperture leaking brown is looking lonesome,

so, knowing you should be the bit of strange
you want to see in the world, I stick my finger into that for a change.

At which the tumbler divides on every issue. I need a tissue; my order
won't take orders. A muddy crystal hysteria, enshrining disaster, redefining borders.

CAMBRIDGE,

this long vac past: a lot of fatty rats
are coming out of bins. They spill as beans
might do when gone to seed, at heightened rates.
The way the Cam's a note, sustaining, bent
below the punter's fretting-finger pole
and granting bluish graces to the meadows
beyond which cranes are necking, on the pull
and town and make, I like. The rats, less so,
although their Chinese year, my year of birth,
could make me think their rising from such trash
indicative, if clumsily, that *reach*
is far from vain, *above* a valid path,
depart a basic sum. But, Xu Zhimo,
it's whom you know, you know? A damn shame, chum.

BRIEF ENCOUNTER

What's wanted's a kiss through the carriage window: eroticised glass buggered
to bits, constellating, twin rhinestone zodiacs rezoning our puckered

mugs. Baby I'm bored on a train. Look, stranger: tunnel vision, lo-fi loupe,
creeping monocular leer. This moment's owed no monument so it's a leap

to be crafting one here. But my fleas, iron-fortified, are micro-forges,
getting busy as my bunnies do. It's phoney because it's true. The law of averages

says you're ón something. The laws of combustion say I'm on fire. Heat me
despite it all! Meet me in the middle of my skull! What should defeat be

but this screed of ungainly keening, this spit of hiss, of grease and fry?
Meaning uncouples from reasonable whys. My fleas and I

aren't justified in our alignment. Talk about trust and I'll tell you where mine went.
But don't. Take note: my will's reproducing to the power of won't.

When matters last were otherwise, a damned city fell. Pretty Helen, witty Nell,
or whoever the hell. I want you so bad in the sense of not well.

WUSSY

Your masseur is a malcontent. Witness
his deigning not to tread on my twig neck
at any opportunity. Frig, heck
– I gotta stick around. A bird flitters

pretty much unnoticed 'bout the station.
Not unimpressive, for the mighty roc.
A less- or greater-than dongle, its beak.
Your masseur is a map of omission.

Nero fiddles, in the US Midwest,
with amp settings. Might each amp be a sun
neatly voiding one civilisation?
The amps' wham is the figurative best,

like your figurative breasts, celeri-
ac lips and all that I'm looking straight at;
shadeless, I'm stumped, pretty much persuaded
and purse-snatched by everything but me.

HELPLESS

A vulgar hope was yours
WILLIAM WORDSWORTH

There is a town in North Ontario,
studies show. I've never yet found Fennario

or found you intriguing, complimentarily speaking.
Your imminent sense of release is leaking

all over your chop shop's fogging countertop.
This vertiginous brain-freeze is the mountains' strop

at yet another couldn't-be calling them a clerestory
with blown blue windows. Let's have an ice-skate amnesty.

Let's not be having you. I am still avenues,
with you, shrill caribou, spoiling my views.

You hate this street? You're beyond the roadside's
assistance. Don't cross without looking at your life

from both sides. Nobody burns at the touch of your man-thing;
you like to say 'dance', but I don't think you're dancing.

GOLDFINCH

for Jack Thacker

Soundbitesize memories belong not to goldfish
but to us, who are probably not goldfish. Cultish

devotion to culling one tiddly square of lichen.
A view not to my liking: goldfinch – nugget-chicken,

cocoa with notes of jam and custard,
candied pine cone built out of a buzzard –

says *Buzz off, biohazard*; won't buzz me in.
An angel's branding-bastard rusting in Edenic rain.

Of the two finches glimpsed in the garden
I can filch no vocab to farewell the gone one.

This other's a bother. Riffling *Some Trees*,
hanging around like wind broken in cemeteries,

picking pinched harmonies to a twig's first snap:
startle, nut, nettle-sting. Snub. Unsatisfied sap.

AS SOON AS I LOVE HER

Beside myself, I'm a waxwork, in the sense of a lava lamp.
No slow-mo yo-yo though: a coffin full of fire. A light for fools.
An iron lung. Lung meaning maiden, where maiden means fil-
ing… Try trilinguistics. Like the excellent shepherd who could never love a lamb

like me. A lamb who's still magnetised and scrapes in His wake.
In part. The part whose rapture takes it so far then hits reverse,
sees it duck-dive slowly flamewards like so much free verse.
Duck-dive slowly flamewards, do its little turn on the catwalk.

And if you're ever more persuaded that I haven't a damn clue
about gods – the conceited sense of gods, the extended metaphor –
I direct your attention to the camp lava river chilling on its killing floor.
I direct your attention to the sunset silhouette of the lamb whose

fleece shears itself and like volcanic smoke curls
to the black domino sky from which stars fall like girls.

AN INTIMATE COMPLAINT

Don't be rash, rash; rash, be not hasty.
Spread not your swan-wings o'er my Leda's rushes;
when my left eye jumps her right eye lashes
me. She treats me sparingly; don't waste me.
Well excuse me while I feng shui the universe
to accommodate your double-parked aura!
There's something impolite behind your arras.
Alas my lass falls victim to your never
and her nerve ends. Some wounds don't mend.
Some moon somewhere's out of place, hold on...
I made a swan out of a poem: fold, un-
fold, organic growth, Bob Mould; I meant
to sail that bird on a puddle swollen with sunset,
but discreet cloud drew the down of itself
over the itchy sky and its blooded lens. Life
floats on, and who needs a swan, or a swan like that?
Not everything is about sex, you know,
which is not to say that this isn't; but little
rash, here is a seed, literally, for your fatal
flower garden: may it be the most that you grow.

DERIDING A HORSE

after Mike Stocks

Slag nag. It's nigh ridiculous that you're
the gall in gallop and the can't in canter,
the sad in saddle-sores on the Infanta,
persisting in your grand vainglory. Lor.

My pro-choice cred looms darkly for you, horse.
How else might mortal poesy document
my sending back your scent, how I resent
your legs' italics limning gooseflesh, gorse –

and now you turn horse sonnet vaulting turn
like milk like moods in rooms unridden turn
like pilot season fold to foal…? Drain-mane,

long-dark-nightmarishly insoluble
won't wash. I wish you rain and ill and gone,
my clip-clop klutz, effaced by space you fill.

PARRHASIUS

for Eric Langley

When Carlia, hair unupbraided,
reviewed that comet's much-missed blink,
the ken of harps could not explain it.
Her eyes were shut. Her shoes were skink.

The peahen with the muff of mink.
The skunk in vellum. I'm the least
enveloped, per my quirky kink.
A minor blot, a minibeast,

a microdot – *Gott*, yesterday
I was, I think, the sharp hot stink
o' Filofax. I like this link:

the thumb-piano plonker's plinks'
pristine drapes flaunt their trompe l'oreille;
you draw them open anyway.

A LIGHT FOR LEONARD COHEN

I believe that I heard my father sing,
when I was seventeen
or so, some lines from 'Master Song'.
Severe, the sovereignty

of his office board room. Today, I assume,
we die, tomorrow love one another;
Auden's 'affirming flame'
in part the agony of *and* or *or*.

A sunbird, plumage bound in smoke,
blinds itself for its night journey.
A poem unread will regardless make
good on its premise. One word, churning.

You: *I would love to see those matches flare.*
The poem: *Thanks for the song, Eliezer.*

RIFF

i.m. Graham Pechey

Torchlight's glissando along the zebra's slideshow side drifts to a discord of
      densening middle-night,
having gone too far, meaning it had gone, at a point, far enough. Now the beam
      gathers into its particular net

neither zebrafish (which, being freshwater denizens, require, it would appear, no
      pinch of salt in their wounds to heal them, no vinegar)
nor quavers lifting from the stripe of antique zither a grifter or similar ne'er-do-
      well might contrive to finagle

from a dealer in stringed instruments, a dealer whose strum-greasy strings
      remained all too easy for said rascal
to pull, but dextrous gestures of the dusty dust that's the zebra's parting's serif,
      and a little air. The zither, primed for resale.

Refrain, from *refrenare*, meaning to apply a bridle. It ill behoves the zebra to
      riffle cards,
behoves it iller still to append 'If I don't do it, who will?' to the Nicene Creed.

The unit of composition less the line or the sentence than, what? The elegy's
      unique derivation no more or less damnable
than the monosyllable *my* slipping from the mantelpiece-high Anglican of,
      whose, *your* funeral?

Refrain, from *refringere*, meaning to break up or break open. In the manner of
    that merely ornamental fox
knocked from the mantel that it might well have figured the roof of the world.
    Put together – or is it *fixed?* –

like a thought. Glue habit in a new habitat, for all I know. Mouthing at a carafe
    of foam. *Refringere*, meaning to refract,
in the manner of the torchlight that skews searingly, it would appear, through a
    hole in water yet leaves the zebrafish, almost explicably, intact.

BLUES FOR ANNIE CLARK

The eagle died on Friday. It did it my way:
ripping to ribbons the regal things the skies say,

felching the flaw out of their argument and retching
that up with the rest of it. I don't believe in reaching

the end of your teething ring. 'Twixt lip and lip
slip not Tippee cup nor toddy but Möbius strip.

And rock a bad body. It's *GTA: San Andreas*'s fault a
boy clips some bystanders leaning into the volta.

Fie! I oughta. I've already swum with dolphins, albeit from
a long way off. Already offered St Vincent half my income.

Still somehow not winning. I want to beat a cheerleader.
Quoth the raven, *It's a crazy feeling when the rooky wood's your larder*,

the rookie mystique notwithstanding, I concur. I'm breaking
pies, dividing conkers. Making misgivings. I'm here for the taking.

II
STUFF

GEAR

after Adrienne Rich

This cocktail stick is the ideal spear
for the floorspace afforded us, here by the pier.
Ditto that toothpick. Ditto my career:
tapered to a point that blunts on a mere

patty of piggy, or the tooth at my ear
where said piggy gets stuck. Compare the dear
little catalogue of failings to the scale of the near-
unscalable heights of their warehouse! I fear

this story is not for us. I'm afraid we veer
from the plot line into a creek of craft beer,
a box set and a mid-range bourbon bringing up the rear.

Hell is other people having one hell of a year.
Heaven is a half rhyme. God is queer.
His list must not have room. Our names do not appear.

HUMANITY

I dream of curing the heels, of blinding the totally lame.
But that'll do, it being half one in the afternoon a.m.

Cease leaving eyelash shavings in the llama cage.
Desist in the wallpapering of our seventeenth couch.

There is no *p* in your trendy modern pneumonia.
There is no small derision. All excisions will own you.

I owe you nine biscuits. You owe me much beeswax
having slain all the bees having sworn they were goshawks.

The plural of saffron, ma bête, is not 'saffrons'.
You're killing actual goshawks now so you plainly know the difference.

Keep looking my gift harpsichord in the mouthguard
and I'll chuck you the gist of my glance prancing southwards:

our great migration to the slimy climes of our incompetence,
with you in the *Hindenburg* and me in the opposite.

SINCERITY

Bare trees in sunlight. Rusted chandeliers.
I can barely bear trees:
wearing out their woodblock batteries
when there'll always be somebody taller

or with more plums. I can barely bear fruit
with its fresh set of problems. All that work,
building bridges in its inner dark,
for what? Everything's fate: oxygenate.

That's whence we've grown this need, no doubt,
to ironise till all ironed out,
roll oxydice across the neutral zone,

betting it gets no better. Always worth a punt,
the die-cast shadows of chandeliers in sun.
Under rust-yellow wallpaper, rust-yellow paint.

WONDERLAND

Frosted window boxes. Such sweet debris
after a collapse,
be it *financial* or *my devastating emotional* or *total moral*.
To everything there is unreason.

Yet a man in a shop on the near corner of January
is moving his lips,
and sound is coming out. What a world.
He apropos of zero announces that the sun,

'we've now determined', is a nuclear explosion.
His brain is a mushroom. It falls out headlong
near the light bulbs; back it bounces. Bounteous Venus

next door puts a coconut shell to her ear, and listens
while he so to speak mars his opener: 'Nothing's gone *wrong…*'
The words console. They're a poem. They needn't convince.

DREAMLAND

Enjoying a big mug of literal tears. Did you know 'utopia' means both
'stop bothering me' and 'seriously, stop'? Give me enough rope

and I'll eat for a day. Give me enough hope and I'll bang myself.
Yet duty makes free calls, and I'm looking into the face of some underdeveloped
    sea life

and trying out the empathy thing. *Tweet tweet tweet, so rudely forc'd.* This roleplay
would suit me because I want to go somewhere. But I knelt there at the Delta

check-in desk and wept at the specificity of the departures.
I went back to the stupid rental and watched a video about a cool Danish archer.

To have you on my dreamland would be like heaven to me. Unfortunately
it's a dreamland where 'snowflake' still denotes any fool who's not a neo-Nazi,

rather than one of these incessantly strobing blips of succour-for-Albion
catching in drifts the kids are thoroughly into. Am I the only one

who doesn't know what I'm talking about? In nightmares, I approach the butthurt.
I glaze what ribs of theirs were spared. I get the honey from their near-bled hearts.

WOMEN

I got a woman. She's so wrecked, she spills my nuts
on the mixing desk. That's a big tiff. I like big butts

of sacerdotal recall: the lad at the pulpit
who puts in his thumbdrive and tells you to suck it.

The body of work is outlined in talk.
I think I mean talc. I think I mean caulk.

I don't really think, as it isn't my favourite
thing to think thoroughly then have to pay for it.

Celibate myself, I singe my shelf with
whinges; my grudge-flushed sponges are bricks.

We've claimed our grief. We've flossed the plot.
I GOT HER I GOT HER I GOT HER I GOT

says the lucre-like tension. Spoils being essential.
I got a woman says the outline aforementioned.

KNIGHT'S WOUNDS WITH EXIT SIGN

She cannot pare him. Snicker-snack,
her charming penknife fouls its bite;
his calcium and magnetite
are loaded, stoked, and push her back

through red-hanged hall and orchard brown.
He magnifies his wounded plight.
They bleed the day, they bleed the night,
his moonlike holes: such ill is born

from wells of know-not-what-I've-done
that – perishing, insurgent – she
would not let *corpus Christi* be,
would witticise and shit thereon

until he, *lully*, full of clay,
should choke on appleseeds, *lulley*.

STUART PEARSON WRIGHT: *THE SPECTRE OF BRAVE ALONZO*

You get the funniest looks from everyone. Your meat
essentialised into cloyingly laughing stock, you're optional mood

lighting installed in the operating theatre. Always late and
better never. Your level of dependency deserves a patent.

You need to get an office job. You put your daddy off his food.
You should walk a mile in your shoes. Or stow your foot

where you shove your money. Yeah, this might be hard for you.
We're kind of busy singing, but we'll spare an hour for you,

then take it from the top and do short shrift and side projects.
Now look who's in the rain-check bin. 'Reanimation' is a bit of a stretch:

you sit and you stand and your helmet squeaks. It isn't all bleak:
you have a better life within you. But it's a maggot. Alas, poor pillock,

   (I know, I know)

you believe, as in the drama of the grave of which you're a recent native,
that by fleeing the chessboard floor you'd be taking the knight off.

STUART PEARSON WRIGHT: *TAKE THE NIGHT OFF*

skulls' mouths
LOUIS MACNEICE

Is she your special lady? In the portrait her instrument's corpse-head yawns.
Women's wrong. Active's right. Night of the living tone-deaf comes on:

in the Dorian mode, the mix mildly erodes; the work's towed; a dove explodes
in an oven. *Darling, you need to toughen up, slap, less lissom, some oxblood*

into your cheeks is what the anatomy's grace is about to receive. The risk of
the compact's mirror's disc skipping, or slipping, a bleed. Get your rocks off

her, diamond geysers, firehosing fairy-light crystal revisions:
set your ears instead to the pealing paint for her audible change of expression.

Of which none. This emotion kills fantasists. This cash-in eats disorders.
This machine's a purged wardrobe, a guitar that will not reattire

the spattered map of her in its clap and shadow. The aesthetic objects
strongly. There's more or less than a woman to meaning so well. But I've checked,

and I am, through all my post-Prufrock one-two talk, still utterly
a sucker for a girl spun of sugar. My people are a loser. Be better for me.

ON MARK HENLEY'S 'NOVEMBER SONG' AS PERFORMED BY THE FLASH GIRLS

What do these women talk about? My poems always failing
the Bechdel test, I expect. I talk about my feelings. Well, my feeling.

I feel well. I feel good. Well, I feel that I should.
I can handle the street. I get out of the woods. I get out

my clauses, which in boggy gloaming loom like the big guns.
Some cattish muse taps MUTE and tries the hedgepig wine.

That hedgepig had it coming. All inner worth must be divulged.
It should make me feel young to look so privileged.

It is, as it were, the autumn of the year. Back home we save our
sectarian burnings for the summer months. But I'm spent as a saver.

Now I own a piece of me: about as much as I can buy.
I'm not a piece of meat. My eyes are all the way

down here, where my hope-upending November song's sphere
of impudence is steamrollering every good wish, as ever.

JOHN CRAXTON: *PORTRAIT OF SONIA* (1948–57)

I understand. A decade blown
to bursting, its glut and its rubberneck gored.
Spinning, from the string of the body's balloon,
between twigs, a skewed grid.

Don't talk. This isn't a poem. Pull on
not forelock but base coat, and wade
out through the pool scummed with pollen.
Be unfallen. Spider, spider, turning white.

Weeds mock a plot arc, a bended knee.
Heartily sorry for having offended thee,
they, as you through your film of noir, see

that there's mostly too much *other* to
make forsaking it fair. Rarely, too,
sufficient *always* to save the face just so.

NEVER GET OLD

However hard I squint at a distant gutter
I can't pretend I'm not on a star. I'm no alligator:

I don't get down amid the dirty and the true.
Not to transcend constantly is all I'm trying to do,

but I default to an idol, aiming for the pew,
ending up the architecture's centre. Bowie,

low thunder, earthed himself between the fall and
the rise, between the milkshakes and the milk float:

it's that Americanophilic Anglocentric quotidian
against which I come off so readily as alien.

My makeup's just made up. I'm acting the actor
when, really, this has always felt real: chugging cups of nectar

up with the lark, coughing up sweet peas and fat green bees.
Such is eternal life and everlasting peace.

These wonders never crease. At the elbows
all is goose feather, goose grease. And no wind blows.

No red brick alley funnels the fussing of sirens.
I've chosen a lengthily happy retirement

of flicking high horses at clueless gas giants
a next world away from nylons and talent.

My milk teeth yielded merrily to pliers, my wisdom
to a drill bit. I won such exits because I wished them.

I grasp contentment. But help me with the pain.
For I have desired to go and put on *Ziggy Stardust* again

and expose what I long thought I wanted veiled,
the nails I evaded and now yearn to get: young, old,

this creature fair. Fighting in Belfast, or anywhere. My share.
My left hand pushing through sharp and sided hail or the market square.

AUGUSTE RODIN: *L'ÉTERNELLE IDOLE*

That seems about right. But perhaps I could simply.
Knock us together our irrespective noggins,
which look not like nuptials nor. Bunnykins,
such discontent requires much disassembly.

As was implicit. Exquisitely kismetic, mes-
meric, mosquitoid. Unfoetid, sun-fettered fleet
buoyed by a depth charge. Keep curtsied
your cursive, its Rorschach-blonde quickness,

and mark but this fleece of relief and alfalfa,
its caramel ballet. The blown sky, thinking on
meteor matters. Than one wan toucan can.

Disfiguring out my angle. My anchor.
I may be a lover but I ain't no. Plans are
what happen while you're making another life.

DISTRIBUTARY

They fork you off them, Mum and
Dad. In the manner of a salmon

you flip out of their union,
expelled from their canon

as pee from a pizzle.
Heffalumps and woozles

mine cellphones for Google
along your banks; the signal

brings the noise and they cum
on felt. Dad's feeling like Mum:

full pelt to the big wet. Wide shot,
dismissal, you've been let

down by the river. Beg not to differ:
you are the great unforgiver.

TWO KOMODO DRAGONS EATING A DOLPHIN

Everybody wave to the dolphin   oh.
That's a blow. Not waving   or drowning.
Perhaps for the happy   couple some *vino*?
Or (forgive the   impertinence) a napkin?

*

After, there'll be a mouth   wash gargle
and all shall be well.   The dolphin's just sleeping
the sleep of the just   eaten. The dragons will kill
only the lights   that live inside everything.

*

Big muscles' blunt muzzles bump   plastic knives in
spaghetti shapes   that might have been letters.
Although we cannot   with confidence version
the cryptozoological augury   the snouts pestle and stir,

the language isn't   unfamiliar. I believe all manner
of thing shall be   … well, a little bit meaner.

WRITING A POEM ABOUT TWO KOMODO DRAGONS EATING A DOLPHIN

I take sides
as if the main meal
were insufficient.
I want all infant

reptiles dead.
I want my fellow
mammal all shined
and resigned

to a full belly
(packed; intact),
to dolphin jubilees
and defiance of a fact.

I salve the whales until
the eyes fall from my scales.

JOHN EVERETT MILLAIS: *THE TWINS, KATE AND GRACE HOARE*

Not to speak of the dog. Not to be difficult.
Not to carve ivory doves in the confines of an ivory dovecote

and toss them from the god-giddily high art of the potence
to feather into eggshell, gifted like a pittance.

I can be your china doll. I don't believe in *I Ching*.
I tune into the frequency of doves or divas cross-hatching,

cross the wires of my purpose with the streamers of my
folly. I learn the smoked-glass tongues of ghosts, immersively.

Not to speak of their father having manufactured that from which an
image, stolen, might be bred. Not to speak of their surname's derivation

from a word meaning boundary, a word meaning white,
and the nothing-left-between-them blackness that might,

should an heir intrusive presume to give – thank you, Grace; all clear, Kate –
the nod, insist that they will not consent, or combine, or separate.

HAMMER HORROR

You can't make an egg without doing something complicated to an omelette.
This *Malleus Maleficarum* has an afterword by the legendary Timmy Mallett,

a selling point that justifies the revival of all manner of sadly archaic activity.
Listen, I'm all for the triumph of reason, but these screams are beyond riveting.

I'm all for one and a man for all seasons. Look like Percy Shelley, feel like Liam
    Neeson.
Cut, like, a buffalo? the scriptures say; to oppose manifest destiny is high treason.

Hammer-wielding I drive them towards the cliff's cut-off. It's more than sheer. It's
    Shakespeare
and his enjambments. The coyote persuaded by the wing of fate to clear

the edge, pause in mid-air, drop catastrophically off-screen… My bleak midwinter
dream come true! I can't make this egg without you. Rhododendrons

pave the road to heaven; I mean to say, I intend to plant them. The herd flows.
They have their times of the month. They have their buffle highs and buffle lows,

and none of them knows: the hammer is paper, tape, yesterday's news of an auto-
    da-fé.
I have put away childish things but not the hero's weapon or the hip hip hooray,

and for the déjà vu of this imminent desolation I am utterly not désolé.
The dust kicked up makes flowering shrubs seem to ghost the last of the day-

light; what looks like a woman must be the dusk egging on, leading astray.
It might be that the chicken quits the cliff and cliff and coyote and all else fall away.

IT FOLLOWS

You're really not my typo. The one in
my first book – unsoundly proofed and glaring

from the distance it keeps constant as
I go about what pass for my days –

sticks out like that trimmed beach body, her
leg reversed and running off the bone. Butchery,

bitches, has thrown off blood on blood.
Bestialitoughtitty. I am in blondes

stepped in so far. 'I Follow Rivers' shivers
in an earphone wire. Her leg refers

to one of the things I walk on best. Deep sea,
baby. The jumbled contents of the chest, the

snarling cove with breakers in its jaws,
must have good reasons. Tread softly, just because.

JUMP SCARE

the death then of a beautiful woman is unquestionably the most poetical topic in the world
EDGAR ALLAN POE, 'THE PHILOSOPHY OF COMPOSITION'

Revved-up red sweet peas rip roaringly through multiple mattresses.
As well they might, chump. Measured out in severed thumbs, the stresses

that fracture facsimile into real art: the beautiful dead girl,
flat on her pamphlet. A spring launch. Have at it. Cure-all

sopped by a blanket. A white heal-all, holding up a banquet.
The Sangreal, the sinkhole; the folio so enthusiastically shanked

that it's earned being speed-read all over, yes indeedy. A beautiful dead
poem, though, comes on so needy. Come up and see me. I'm insulted.

I'm inured to feeling unsure of this having purchase within my purview
is the sort of statement I'm inclined to undercut. Feverfew

is another thing, in the vein of the chapbook that's gore-sodden,
garlanded. Suspicious of the sell-by of what's new, raw, sudden,

let's, I and I, abide in the room in the tower, making next to nada happen.
A blank state. A white cell. Then a hand that's far from ours turns the sanguine
     tap on.

III
FUTURES

SCENES FROM THE PARISH

I

The spectacle's lenses regrind themselves.
In disco sunlight, quail shadow the fields,
manifold, defiant. See their long swarm
blow shapes from rain and the charlatan earth.

Soon. Dry harvest moon. Its virtue furnace.
Rodents, darting wide of timber chambers,
refine a deafening reel. Ah! Uproar.
The gentleman had wanted for music.

Lyric I padlocks Jesterface to mud,
that he might force roots and raise a forest
in this briefest of all longevities,

while in gardens shudder little children,
caught in their knots, cooped in their cubicles.
Such lines seem an intelligent sickness.

11

Inadequate salt. Crude surfeit of wolves.
An observer gasps, can henceforth relax:
the college green, bracketed by gutters,
shows tedious dramas nearing a close.

The sweet proposal becomes a habit
in office life. Ask any immune aunt,
or show a smashed diplomat the fountain.
Distant fires offset the surly cobbles.

We plunge so nobly for bland compassion,
quips Jesterface; I doesn't get it up.
Crabs harass dentists in windows. Embox

soft Katherine, who must not witness funds
removed from knotholes be applied slapdash
to barristers, to terminals, to joys.

III

Eli, ho-hum, clamours for calamine,
blunt as an England fan. It is inferred
he has confused a stained colonial
tract and his school's savage dormitory.

Lean rather hard with your clean consensus
and phage from page might be for good unrhymed.
Damp fur dresses intricate wardrobe walls,
donning moth-thought and projection, whereas

a crow flattens to a drafted quaver
in the signifyin' cataract. Ouch.
Come in, Arlene, from the tempest and thyme,

for night is dawning: guts and black cotton.
Quite tender noise slinks yet from the wormhole.
I's in the red. Jesterface in the cloud.

PEDAL STEEL

for John Clegg

The liquidy slide scrolls through a timeline.
A birth and some stuff and a death ago
across Searle Street, Veronica Forrest-Thomson
is buffering *On the Periphery*

presumably via looking at it straight on.
You do what you must do. Satan,
your kingdom must come down.
I must spend my days doing something.

Which must be like looping a dolly-zoom
shot of a train unmoved in a station.
It crosses into the room, it seems.
This feels like a bad naturalisation,

but how could you not think about hands,
fingers, feet, the thereness of your knees?
Doesn't a studied extension beyond
the artwork shade back into artifice,

emotion's correspondence with precision
being what the cherry-faced picker's perfected?
You don't lock the case and hand the keys in
having posted into history your aural factoid:

not to petrify into loathsome cliché,
but you persist, lonesome, on edges. *My great danger
is to talk about literature
as if it were all poetry.* It's poker, it's ouija;

it's houses and widgets. You swipe
right and left. The vehicle remains
in a stopping position, and yet. *I also hope
though don't quite see how at the moment.*

MIRRORBALLS

I couldn't get any beakers. I'd have kept
my acid in mid-air, but the swishly swept
floor implored so. Jeepers wept.
To the blackning church, totes apols.
Likewise its basement, home of mirrorballs.

To each there is a purpose: namely, to distract
a light-beam from its penitential focus
and make it make significance for locus upon locus.
TO BE CONFIRMED on every blue plaque.
'To be brutally honest…' says the overworked claque.

Mirrorballs spritzing the gist of the now.
Poetry: less than just BIFF! BAM! POW!
In meadow, we can build snowplough.
See cow make move on indifferent sow.
See my little ducks, all in a row. *Row.*

Poetry learns you how to say things.
Poetry learns you: flapping your grey wings
sings a consequential rainbow. Alternative
refracts and learns you how to live.
You might want to spend more time bathing.

You might want to read with greater attention.
Dad's still banking on the law conversion
printing C-notes. I shopped for maraschinos
just to watch him die. Trained as a me-surgeon.
Administered saline, to keep the sea low.

Stainless steel stole the show; then they cast iron.
I came to the altar with leading questions.
Often I pray and do so in passing.
When you pass a beached humpback you blubberneck.
You blub for a bit, then snack on the wreck.

I confess I tried to resurrect the beast.
How much of a drag could Leviathan be?
Now the sepulchres are soiled by my doing my least,
dead mirrorballs throwing shade like it's panties.
Over my ruckus, I can scarcely hear Dante

treble firewood in the dead of life, Panzer-filled
Plath polish her final stanza till
she sees her head in its compound eye. This drug
likes pretty. This lustre likes lack. The blood
that blackens these tracks won't talk back.

SLUGS

the sky flashes, the great sea yearns
JOHN BERRYMAN

The slug drifts from the ocean through space. As creatures do.
I take it in my grip. Others take it in the chest, I know,
or as pretext. A drone moans from the featureless blue.
A good sun in the stove of the sky. A pitiless, pilotless glow.

The evacuated street seethes in its carpet of slugs.
Glaucus atlanticus by the gross: arsenic candles
by way of memorial. The human body's a fumble of cogs
less armoured than armorial. A doodle on a sandhill.

The sight has the aroma of glaucoma when you sniff it.
The smell of the smile of the Prime Minister is the reek of
something reloading. That man is a private
island. We none of us have relatives to speak of.

One could do worse, is the horror. Some skirt
so close to the reactor that their special feelings melt.
And after a while the palmed slug can't properly hurt.
Its starship navigates the suicide belt.

Slug, you're the galaxy you cross and the gallows you're dragging!
You needn't reciprocate my wondering what you are.
It's life, friends: a glitch to which we've hitched our wagon,
a wagon worn to wreckage by that blundering star.

Life, friends: a swinger of birches, or morning stars. Counter-terror
before it hatches. The human hand, fully armed: a nail bomb.
Sail on, silver slug; steer by that firmamental error
so glaring that verily it hinders our negotiations.

The lasso of two lacerations, the heavenly outtake
takes a molehill out with a laser. The super blooper's beams are
contractually binding, penned in the demotic
in the future perfect. A footnote slips in. A miserere.

There isn't air enough. I slough off erythema
in the aspect of a dreamer, quaff folderol and oestrogen,
drinking what I can't touch. The blood of the redeemer.
Slug, the gleaming pads of my fingers are you-stricken.

The wrist's second hand is ticking. It elevates you to the light
that is, from an angle, lifting you to me, such that you're between
me and the light in this flicker-failed night and our drought-
clouded eyes swallow us until the light has nothing to see.

PLOT TWIST

Tough luck
You're kidding yourself
SIGRID

Greek fire vommed from a well hard ship.
Neat move, hot shot. Chip

off the blocked users: frost from the boroughs,
tasty shaves from post-organic döner.

Can't put the great back in GBH?
Oh gee, queen bee. Can't hatch

a plot in the pampas grass grown
for patching up empaths? Come

build in the empty
house of austerity:

the full house, empty from
the outside, at a distance, swishly framed,

where the switchblade twist is you lose your name
in the crowd in it, in the spritzed mist of quicklime.

FUGITIVE RHYME

Look it up, fuzzball: Han Solo seems bigger
the farther he falls through the dark.
I'm terrified less by the shell than the trigger,
by the current more than the shark:

finger and thumb, electric razor
– I'm armouring me 'gainst the former.
Beware the damsel who only plays her
dulcimer as a warm-up.

She's perfectly not what you thought she was.
Kellyanne ain't no inspector.
Richard Kimble shears his fuzz
and becomes a famous actor.

And maybe up in the great who-knows
we'll all have chins as polished
as the bust of pug-nosed Bellicose,
or the doll of one-armed Knowledge

draping a daisy chain over a barrel,
installing the router of evil.
Look to that heaven when Munich Beer Hall
Putsch comes to shovel.

The arc of losing readers goes
like this: the Force, the fit,
the quicksand, then the poetry bros
patrolling their patronised myths.

I didn't kill my wyvern. Think
your basilisk's a goner.
Everything's bots. The bathroom sink's
AI's okay, Your Honour,

but, when the chaff's chopped from my visage
to chime with the minging bowl,
I wish I could quit that watery passage
to sinking in clouds of gold.

Fine, the form's transparent. Next.
How tragicomically fecund
this hall that magnifies and reflects
my guiltily difficult background.

Daddy a boy! Mummy a girl!
Conflicted and fickle and bored,
I shave and I crave and feel more of the world
and less of a Harrison Ford.

MAX RICHTER: *SLEEP*

A further verse to waking, if it pleases sir.
A sun all nosy-fingered squeezes her

breast – matters it which? – through an
all-seeing blind and a bra sky is not bluer

than, nor might be. A Heathrow
flight path – matters it? – grants some *teatro*,

each pterosaur snore a slow snare
in the marching band that dares go there:

a plagiaristic gull being sent down, probably;
banter and roast; the traditional cross baby.

Windows yawn; with breezy rage, rails
snooker on frames. At a space-age crawl

the baby goes, electric, into the bathtub
of this white room where hours are racked up.

POEM IN WITCH HAZEL

It slobs on a pillow of shrub or in slime, not making a living.
I hope. I never. 'Poem in Witch Hazel' when ablaze: the thing

wherein I'll con the catchiness you bring; the poem as a salve
for the wounds of its birth. And meanwhile back on planet Earth… Self-

fulfilling property owner coming to me live and messily, I'm
loving what you've done with your nouveau mausoleum

– how don't you sleep? How does it feel like a royalty cheque, 'feel'
being a verb common among one's public? Time will tell just who has fell

deeds to undiddle. I fiddle while bones turn in turf, while persons
percolate in their urns… Yes! The poem burns. Its monkish private arson

drifts from the cloister, lays too-late siege to little stars. The automatic
writer – stuffed parrot; taxing dermatology – chokes indisposed in the attic.

Brightness falls from the error. The mic drops from the trebuchet.
You 'had fun getting to know' me, which suggests you didn't manage it.

OF PARTING DAY

A farting spray: the ocean's flies,
unbuttoned or untoothed, advance
their shame against the ebb, the iv-
ory and orts of meat sans feels.

I sigh, and stalk in high dismay
my tower of dead elephants
and look out on your tower of live
kilometres of wave away.

Diverse alarms and doves all set,
I ring the bell whose neck is wrung,
whose mouth is soft with Nelly dung.
Kilometres of waving jet.

We're born to build. We die to spill.
The curfew tolling love, zip, nil.

ULSTER POET

Trainers aren't walking boots; now they're not nothing. Maybe you
should drive all night just to buy back my bluetoothed baby shoes.

If you're able to believe a single air-dropped pamphlet
then – correct? – comes photos-food-speeches-photos-cèilidh-food.

The wisdom of Crow Jane. Hits recital umpteen; is like,
she'll no longer shred for the part the star charts say she should.

God's in his heaven, so I'll stay in mine. Dirty looks cross
these bomb-blasted lawns, the fecked fence a cairn of naily wood.

Inconsistent gardener flaunts his allotted vices.
He needs to escape! Which gives him this day his daily bruise.

Here's how constant disavowal sounds. *Well I've caught some more
downtime on Beechlands, Queen's Elms, Holyrood.* Upscale weeds ooze.

Such is the room for testing your tongue on the vibing brick
that for Crumbthings licks truer than a soft-serve *save me* could.

ON CRUMBTHINGS

CREATION

Full of promise means full of breakage. Under the thumb?
More like enveloping it: the toy donkey's twangy nerve losing
verve, quadruped snapshot developed as woodpile. The uppercut
suckerpunch, candid take from below that fells you because you
don't want to be raised. Goosed, chaste in laboured pointillism,
the timekeeper Crumbthings, tinderbox crammed with eggs
kinder than so recursive a monotreme deserves, digs pouring-
pores into a prosy garden, plopping in ovoid after samey ovoid.
Semi-avid. Some are fertilised, some become fertiliser first; he
cares but scarcely, by far preferring line-laying. He stares out of
his league. The whites pool in embarrassment.

RUNT

Contents: one use of one impractically unforgivable word.
Needlework needs a little worm. Turn, turn. Hitting RETURN
without reflection makes the grubbiest grumble profound. Nice
pins. But observe the colossus Crumbthings, dancing solo not
on the head but on the point of exclamation! On the point of
starvation, on the point of the revelation that whenever he specifies
he's taken as speaking in general. That whenever he skewers a
universal it's transposed into niche perversion. Nasturtium, trap
crop, hears tragedy cripple-trip over his helmet, his harness, his
crib. Notes down a honk, parses a bleat. Cheat codes are in his
blood.

UMBILICUS

Quite small Freya; smaller fray latching frantic onto passing notions, passing noble gases. Strawberry bootlace blustering from a cutlass's flashy anti-fleshy en dash, huffing at swish brick houses under a face all howl – best mime of its me generation. Yoking your jaundiced cab to a coupla cats's all very well but they are charging towards you. Chariot can't be taken back, crumples accordingly. The surveyor Crumbthings: ruminating on ruin, whipping cats with catgut, spilling children that spoil the road when ridden rudely over. Rips man-size tissue for his pansy issues. Meant to be busy being born and he isn't even trying.

MOB

At length I heard a ragged noise and mirth. Howdy doo, buttermilk squirt; guess you're part of the formless, the homily garbed in pew. What, rough beast? Speak much more loudly if you whoop. Some faraway land has hacked your cough; hush-a-bifurcated lullaby says never be restful, never wake. All they all want is to hold you. Standard teddy bear practises comebacks, nose-and-thumb attacks. Who trashes the attachment? Who warps the warble? Perchance the healer Crumbthings, berthed in the berry and swarth of claw and tooth's redo-do-do-doings. Harpbreaker. Lord of the dense in lion's clothes. *Straighten your suit* attempts Dad, dung-tied.

BETROTHED

Sound a trumpet: a sunflower's the sum of its parps. Prolapses damn if you're doomed, damn if you're doped. An expression of some courage. A marriage of some necessity, you and your precious innards, a bilingual phrase coined at the hip or kinda like approx thereabouts. Do you have the wrung cloth? Eiderdownfall. Heliossify. Punters mouth you without the suggested cadence, with gestures more broad than a wayside, an obscene bean. Kindly unrelax, empty reliquary. Please withhold. The call of nature is very impotent to us. The mime Crumbthings screams hisself stiff, a swizzle stick in a sauna amid dissipating cubes.

TITHE

Self-assessment form stapled to a wrong-size shoebox, horned into which: three creepsakes smashed by three sick smooches; fourteen honest perseverances to preserve fourteen emotional states, each of which has seceded; solo cotton bud chewed to its argumentative scalps. Wax upstreaming. Half hazard, half hesitation, the romancer Crumbthings submits his bin of runoff and run-on sententiousness to the nemesis, he is after all in the sleeper's hold. Hall of poisson, hall of liqueur. By night the duvet's pinched by devil, shade, bug; restored near dawn though by seraphim in sheets' clothing, such that subsequent aubadinage postulates the late knockout was anecdotally fair.

HIGH

The nomad is a Three Mile Island, a lethal particle, and when you touchdown the effectivisation of brawnstormed goal-orientalism you'll find such mortal drift mainly welcome. A bindleful of jargon. Beware the shuttlecock, my stunner. Bluntly, you're a vision in blindness, a slight against the saurian: inhaling Hail Marys or forging a headset, you're a room, temperate. Overlooking a chronic pond. Damselflies are wireless, these days, pinkeens likewise remarkable. Annoying bonsai hands out leaflets to the sadly passed. Free lunch persists. The bartender Crumbthings feels good somewhere about him and cannot put what would, medically, be considered a finger on it.

INTELLIGENCE

Breathing this pollen grants the wisdom of anemones, mon anomie. Should stones cry out, the judge will hang gravel; should oceans cavil, vapour will be gassed. Hunky John Dory gored for the sins of the *Pequod*; grass for a planet's sake garotted by a garotting squad. Trepan the cheesecake pinup. Painfrieze. Innuendover and over: have one on me, one under, and we're done. The invigilator Crumbthings presses squall-like ear to glass, glass to dividing wall. Were the glass in larger pieces, the overheard slander would to a lesser extent smart. Were the ear a body else's, it would, post-hate, post-haste withdraw.

NUGGET

Immaculation crisis averted, every deconvert in town saddles up a perfunctory review. After the advertised guilt rose a glorious unburdening, now a cummerbund for the nurse Crumbthings, picking his pretty path among the graves like a firework in a petshop. Commercial jets' perpendicularity, snailing on nimbostratus a cruciform transfer. Gorgeous gorges. See how the weasel is a jolly whistling sort. Consider how the enemy in hell is the perambulator of art. The house a deferred discussion. The garden an unsolicited tip. A clamp on the tree. Nettles in the Rorschach. Make like a sheepdog and get the flock out of here.

GAUZE

The helmet's well metal. Beyond the chapeau of redoubt, the blindfold's the hottest for how it holds your eyebrows in. *Got some more gossamer, guv'nor* says the craftspersonality. Performance pottery goes everywhere. Cleverest trick being to shun the hazy cells of one's surrounds, attending to the fibrous filter's capillaries. Aunt Sally's ancillary in her pencil-skirting boredom; the bupkissing cousin's hard as carousels, splooshing about. Noon sinks into the futon of forgetting. The orator Crumbthings has clothes but no cigar, as in his gob's freed up to whiterabbit drunkpunchingly onwards and the congregants have no manna of devastating vision to distract them.

SANITY

Crosses burning on ballot papers; thistledown carved into foreheads. Valuable moments of pastoral sincerity occur amid shorted cirruses. Why look: the pylons are ants, atlases, Atlanteans. A vote of no continents. The ocean takes the floor, the walls go whaling, and the ceiling whacks the navigator Crumbthings, his pockets maligned with syllable and goad. This idea is a wee bit zany. This IKEA siege equipment requires collaboration but no training. This is the optimum view of our beloved capital, which is the booster seat of power, the ejector seat of endurance, the deceit of our classic bants, and just the worst.

NOVA

No vanity mirror, in which is espied no vamp. The no bulbs must be thoroughly and expensively pulped for the troubled print industry. The gambler Crumbthings enters a soirée as might a pinball table be quit by its eponym: fiddling flippers, fatter than lychees, trying to unhappen it. Trifles eaten from apostrophes, fig skewers from fiddlesticks; yonder the contralto, making a significant contribution to her hors d'œuvre. That guest is the meatless metonym. In thee, no veritas. In greenery outside, patterns demur, one assumes, else what sport in this saleable imposition? It is orefully close. You gasp the concept concrete imagines.

Epiphany packs sidearms only strolling to the local. The route is paved with gut infections, with god dilations. Ambidecorous ambient heterocore glazes tables in the private rumour-milking shed, while quires of rowan wrap clingily around fab statuary. The observation seeks the purpose to which its truth is sufficient. The undertaker Crumbthings seeks the prepossession that might curate some time in the Agnus Dei. Innocent vectors, the arrangements that effect the sleeping body's progressive convulsing; rounds of vultures, the crotchets stitched into the air only slightly above, no-deals pacing the eye of the semibreve. Out, out, brief case in which we trust.

★

I'm a black starfish, says a white starfish. It don't matter. Hedgehogs and eagles swap jobs; cacti and lactase bunk up. There is an acoustics to identity. There are choruses to identify. The music of the sufferers, heaven at its darkest an intricate scheme… The implosion Crumbthings, squatting squeamishly over the throne of his dead, appearing from afar to be sitting: subservient, unchilled, a nib tethered a hairshirt's breath from the paper; a fountain of redaction, plugged with a wire. So much right to refuse; so little left to guzzle. Starvation is clutter. Nomenclature's staved in. Catcher in the surf. Stop.

NOPE

Try or try not, there is no do.
Auld triangle. Dew-soft shoe.
I think that I might say achoo
should Lao Tzu drop the soap.

Pressure got the drop on you
who fell in line at sixty-two
with Nancy in her stockings, who
wouldn't, weirdly, cope.

The Spanish fly. The Spanish flu.
The Irish border. Irish stew.
Fake it big or shake it new.
Make it dazzling taupe.

Summer loving happens, true.
Some are born to fling the poo.
Some deer are trees and several Jews
and one an antelope.

I won't speak for the caribou
who let me stay a night. A few.
The boogie blames it on the booze
that blames it on the dope.

Frostier than empires grew
the vale where rot and roses woo.
I sense the import deeply through
my cockeyed telescope.

Holy Father, please excuse
my irremediable views.
I catch your webcast, bank of rue,
and send the Pope a grope.

The petals on a wet bough blues;
the currency we can't but use.
Leave your hack on, Mammon. Strew
some slippers on the slope.

Sunken in the cud that chews
the inhalations of the moos,
I have my fill and yet refuse
the offer of a rope.

Whisht your moping, Mary Sue.
If you knew. Oh if you knew.
Here it is, son: do, or do
not. There is no hope.

NOTES AND ACKNOWLEDGEMENTS

Earlier, some might say the earliest, versions of these poems were composed in the womb. That one cuddling womb. The pregnancy's spontaneous termination facilitated my rendering them fit for human engagement, redrafting them as less transcendentally cruel.

The flowing publications: oceanthology, bloodpamphletting, streams.

Eleven of the references to my childhood in a haunted island lighthouse are true. The other three are true also, but are about *your* childhood in a haunted island lighthouse. You don't remember. Mercifully, given which three.

Nor had I thought that perishing in so humiliating a fashion before birth would facilitate a childhood, or the authorship of 'Notes and Acknowledgements' and allegedly more besides, but here we very much are. *Jubilate uh-oh.*

The first word that comes to mind upon reading each of these pieces contributes to a reverse acrostic offering the location of the terrible nameless city where I sit, most months all years, reflecting in anguish upon your having no idea how difficult that was to pull off. And upon the neighbours: their eyelessness, their orthodontics, their attempts at infiltration. I cannot recommend visiting. But please.

Don't start me on the interplay of definite and indefinite articles. It was so nuanced, its binary language expressive of the ludic, the gnomic, a carnal. I lost my tracks; I kept *editing*...

Italics are *not* indicative of a failure of nerve in the face of creative procedures' unsought revelations.

You don't look like the sort of person who buys into phrenology.

I suppose none of them is a proper sonnet.

Dedicating a poem to somebody is not, in the main, analogous to pointing at them, in the camera's backhanded epileptic smack, with both index fingers. Imagine arrowing middle fingers at your chest tattoo of said person, as you fall through the twinkling skylight onto the quiet family.

For the black-market pet trade the venom has the venom removed from its venom. Docility is a sign that the venom is afraid.

Rhymes are fractal. Or fractured. Or frictional; or fatuous. (I should have made a note of this sooner.)

What you are makes no difference. I thank my lurking larking stars.

Poetry is language slowed down to make it harder to understand.

THE BEST POEM

A run of outlines,
like the zoo in a snake. Like
whatever silhou-
etiquette suggests is best
is. Rained offcuts' shadows baulk.

Here's my glockenspiel.
Herewith seafowl, politely
hailed. I message them
from the core of my crumbled
abode in the dark green dark.

I want light green light.
I've misread terns of address.
Editing's the art:
part desperation; largely
excising dedications.

Words flail. Feedback slips.
Yellow faxes reminisce:
secure skies, sound clouds.
Louder than actions, the speck
to which the dreck has declined.

From the submarine
to the meticulous; to
the handed baton
from the thumb war, the sketch in
flame and nail: dream vacation.

Traumatic day trip.
The consistency of tone
is bad for wading.
No question of evading
what moves with such suddenness.

No sense engaging
what moves with such certainty:
I seen a corpse fly
abrade a city-wide hull
with greater efficacy.

Goodness atrophies
in a harness. The honest
sympathies vibrate
is what I've convinced myself.
I have prior convictions.

Not funny tra-la.
Attacks return. Queues are flubbed.
Hubbub when the clash
registers. Spending out loud.
Like funny pecunious.

Earth has nothing to
chauffeur it. Throw a Grecian
urn or two. I miss
you happens in the breast of
folk. The rest is counterpart.

Counterpoint: finger
paints; having writ, tows lies of
least resilience
into the great white's open
submission. Prophetic? Nah.

No aesthetic but
autobiographical-
isthenics. Confess-
ionull hypothesissies.
Sunset in foam: roe, boys, roe.

It does not adhere.
Sixty sexts per second, sir.
My strobing punches:
Le Penseur. Taylor tinkers
with solder. Saudade's nice.

The sonar's so good
my heel taps to what enwraps
the vessel. Beep, click:
this beat is sick. It must die.
Lorde, have mercy upon us.

JOHN SINGER SARGENT: *CARNATION, LILY, LILY, ROSE*

for Ros

I tender a posy of vaccination bruises,
a tense neutrality of wafer, an atomic
waste of forget-me-pleases. The jackdaw raises
the matter of the backlog. Too much
inflammation, girlfriend. *Calm down*'s derivative.

How the hue of the conventionally precious
is cued to chill and dim by its core endive.

Which hence radiates. This little pigment races
something dark to a shady bank. Sika, ye
shall find ye locked in oneupmanship
with dappled surrounds; shall deepen hence, such

as one might, as one up and quits
– vacillating, bursting – Vauxhall for Brixton,
expound on what it is the lights are tricks of.

'Damae Plures': The title was the most acoustically pleasing Latin translation of my first book's title, *Several Deer*, that I could devise. The poem ended up doing its own thing and having a different rhyme scheme, but it was conceived as a tribute to Geoffrey Hill's 'Lachrimae', to which I often returned in the course of the writing, although 'I hole up in the culture of my stuff' versions Leonard Cohen's 'stuff it up the hole in your culture' from 'The Future'.

'Deriding a Horse': This is a version of Mike Stocks's 'Describing a Horse'; I wrote it as part of a short talk on Stocks's poem for Poetry in Aldeburgh 2018.

'Parrhasius': Parrhasius took part in a painting contest with Zeuxis, who features in Eric Langley's poem 'Glanced'. *Carlia parrhasius* is the fire-tailed rainbow skink.

'Riff': Echoes of Roy Campbell's 'The Zebras' are mostly intentional.

'Gear': The final sentence of this poem resembles the final line of Adrienne Rich's 'Diving into the Wreck'.

'Dreamland': The title and the sentence featuring it are from a song by Bunny Wailer that closely versions 'My Dream Island' by The El Tempos.

'Women': The repetition of 'I GOT HER' is from Levan Gabriadze's film *Unfriended*.

'Knight's Wounds with Exit Sign': This version of the Corpus Christi Carol hasn't, to the best of my knowledge, any significant connection beyond its title to Ocean Vuong's *Night Sky with Exit Wounds*.

'It Follows': The typo in my first book involved 'bestiality' appearing as 'bestitality'. The title and the central image are from David Robert Mitchell's film *It Follows*.

'Jump Scare': The bloody-mattress image is from Ben and Chris Blaine's film *Nina Forever*.

'Pedal Steel': The italicised portions, '*On the Periphery*' aside, are from Veronica Forrest-Thomson's 19 August 1974 letter to G.S. Fraser, as published in *Jacket*.

'Poem in Witch Hazel': The title nods to *Poems in Which*, to which I would have submitted the poem had I completed it before the journal bowed out.

'Ulster Poet': Formally this is a version of the ghazal, replacing rhyme-plus-repetition with trisyllabic rhyme.

'On Crumbthings': The name of this faltering ego was years ago concocted for some E.E. Cummings pastiches as a fusion of Cummings's surname and mine; I was told subsequently that in German 'krumme Dinge' are dodgy actions, shady dealings, grifts, fiddles, thefts.

ACKNOWLEDGEMENTS

Acknowledgements are due to the editors of the following publications, in which a number of these poems, or versions thereof, first appeared:

Abridged; Eborakon; The Honest Ulsterman; Luminous, defiant; Magma Poetry; The Manchester Review; The North; Pain; Poetry Ireland Review; The Renga Bus; The Rialto; The Scores; Southword; The Tangerine.

Thanks also to the Girton College poetry group and the Cambridge salon/workshop crew for their patience with often very early drafts, and for their insight, support and good company. Extra love and gratitude to Rebecca Watts with respect to same. And secret handshakes to Susannah Dickey and Caoilinn Hughes.